Conquer Your Chaos Planner

This Planner belongs to:

_____

Investing in yourself is a wonderful, life–changing experience, but the process can also be overwhelming. When I first realized how important it was to invest in me, I had no clue how much was truly involved. I often wanted to throw in the towel because I was pushing past my comfort zone and it was challenging in ways I can not even put into words. With time I learned to develop a system that has literally propelled me on the path to success. With my system I realized the importance of creating a routine and planning regularly. The discipline of changing my day to day actions has had a wonderful outcome on my life. I feel more inspired to go after my dreams each and every day. This is what I want for you!

The Conquer Your Chaos Planner was created to help women who are tired of the chaos in their life. This chaos could include frustration with your day to day schedule and overwhelm with the thought of falling short in reaching your goals.

This Planner will provide encouragement, motivation support and organization to set you up for success. This planner is desgined to help you to keep all of your thoughts, goals, and ideas in one place, and helps you to keep track of your writing process. The Conquer Your Chaos planner was created to help you to truly conquer your chaos with ease!

Be sure you take advantage of using this planner daily in order to set yourself up for success.

About the Author

Nicolya Williams is a certified personal development coach, radio show host and best selling author for busy women teaching them to turn their message into their masterpiece. As a coach Nicolya divides her time between blogging, empowering women one on one, and motivating groups of women through masterclasses. To reach her audience Nicolya enjoys mentoring women through her own stories and books. She believes her experiences are from God to encourage women all over the world. Nicolya, a lifelong learner, strives to continue her personal growth through reading and interacting with her social and spiritual community. She is an avid reader and is devoted to building up her own strong women; her two daughters Kaelyn and Kamryn. You can connect with Nicolya at www.nicolyawilliams.com or on all social media platforms @nicolyawilliams.

START DATE

_____

END DATE

_____

Month/Year:

Sunday	Monday	Tuesday	Wednesday	Thursday	Friday	Saturday

Month/Year:

Sunday	Monday	Tuesday	Wednesday	Thursday	Friday	Saturday

Month/Year:

Sunday	Monday	Tuesday	Wednesday	Thursday	Friday	Saturday

My Vision Board

DATE: _____

TODAY'S GOALS:

_____
_____
_____
_____
_____
_____

MUST DO LIST:

_____
_____
_____
_____
_____
_____
_____
_____

TIME	AM PLAN
12	
1	
2	
3	
4	
5	
6	
7	
8	
9	
10	
11	

NOTES:

_____
_____
_____
_____
_____
_____

POWER-HOUR-INTENTIONS:

_____
_____
_____
_____
_____
_____

TODAYS WINS:

TIME	PM PLAN
12	
1	
2	
3	
4	
5	
6	
7	
8	
9	
10	
11	

INTENTIONAL LEARNING:

DATE: _____

TODAY'S GOALS:

_____
_____
_____
_____
_____

MUST DO LIST:

_____
_____
_____
_____
_____
_____
_____

NOTES:

_____
_____
_____
_____
_____

TIME	AM PLAN
12	
1	
2	
3	
4	
5	
6	
7	
8	
9	
10	
11	

POWER-HOUR-INTENTIONS:

_____
_____
_____
_____
_____
_____

TODAYS WINS:

_____
_____
_____
_____
_____

INTENTIONAL LEARNING:

_____
_____
_____
_____
_____
_____

TIME	PM PLAN
12	
1	
2	
3	
4	
5	
6	
7	
8	
9	
10	
11	

DATE: _____

TODAY'S GOALS:

_____
_____
_____
_____
_____
_____

MUST DO LIST:

_____
_____
_____
_____
_____
_____
_____

TIME	AM PLAN
12	
1	
2	
3	
4	
5	
6	
7	
8	
9	
10	
11	

NOTES:

_____
_____
_____
_____
_____
_____

POWER-HOUR-INTENTIONS:

_____

_____

_____

_____

_____

_____

_____

TODAYS WINS:

TIME	PM PLAN
12	
1	
2	
3	
4	
5	
6	
7	
8	
9	
10	
11	

INTENTIONAL LEARNING:

DATE: _____

TODAY'S GOALS:

_____

_____

_____

_____

_____

MUST DO LIST:

_____

_____

_____

_____

_____

_____

NOTES:

_____

_____

_____

_____

_____

_____

TIME	AM PLAN
12	
1	
2	
3	
4	
5	
6	
7	
8	
9	
10	
11	

POWER-HOUR-INTENTIONS:

_____

_____

_____

_____

_____

_____

_____

TODAYS WINS:

TIME	PM PLAN
12	
1	
2	
3	
4	
5	
6	
7	
8	
9	
10	
11	

INTENTIONAL LEARNING:

DATE: _____

TODAY'S GOALS:

_____
_____
_____
_____
_____

MUST DO LIST:

_____
_____
_____
_____
_____
_____

TIME	AM PLAN
12	
1	
2	
3	
4	
5	
6	
7	
8	
9	
10	
11	

NOTES:

_____
_____
_____
_____
_____
_____

POWER-HOUR-INTENTIONS:

_____
_____
_____
_____
_____
_____

TODAYS WINS:

_____
_____
_____
_____
_____
_____

INTENTIONAL LEARNING:

_____
_____
_____
_____
_____
_____
_____

TIME	PM PLAN
12	
1	
2	
3	
4	
5	
6	
7	
8	
9	
10	
11	

DATE: _____

TODAY'S GOALS:

_____
_____
_____
_____
_____
_____

MUST DO LIST:

_____
_____
_____
_____
_____
_____

NOTES

_____
_____
_____
_____
_____
_____

TIME	AM PLAN
12	
1	
2	
3	
4	
5	
6	
7	
8	
9	
10	
11	

POWER-HOUR-INTENTIONS:

_____

_____

_____

_____

_____

_____

TODAYS WINS:

_____

_____

_____

_____

_____

_____

INTENTIONAL LEARNING:

_____

_____

_____

_____

_____

TIME	PM PLAN
12	
1	
2	
3	
4	
5	
6	
7	
8	
9	
10	
11	

DATE: _____

TODAY'S GOALS:

_____
_____
_____
_____
_____
_____

MUST DO LIST:

_____
_____
_____
_____
_____
_____

NOTES:

_____
_____
_____
_____
_____
_____

TIME	AM PLAN
12	
1	
2	
3	
4	
5	
6	
7	
8	
9	
10	
11	

POWER-HOUR-INTENTIONS:

_____
_____
_____
_____
_____
_____
_____

TODAYS WINS:

_____
_____
_____
_____
_____

INTENTIONAL LEARNING:

_____
_____
_____
_____
_____

TIME	PM PLAN
12	
1	
2	
3	
4	
5	
6	
7	
8	
9	
10	
11	

DATE: _____

TODAY'S GOALS:

_____
_____
_____
_____
_____

MUST DO LIST:

_____
_____
_____
_____
_____
_____
_____

NOTES:

TIME	AM PLAN
12	
1	
2	
3	
4	
5	
6	
7	
8	
9	
10	
11	

_____
_____
_____
_____
_____
_____

POWER-HOUR-INTENTIONS:

_____
_____
_____
_____
_____
_____

TODAYS WINS:

_____
_____
_____
_____
_____

INTENTIONAL LEARNING:

_____
_____
_____
_____
_____
_____

TIME	PM PLAN
12	
1	
2	
3	
4	
5	
6	
7	
8	
9	
10	
11	

DATE: _____

TODAY'S GOALS:

_____
_____
_____
_____
_____

MUST DO LIST:

_____
_____
_____
_____
_____
_____
_____

NOTES:

_____
_____
_____
_____
_____
_____
_____

TIME	AM PLAN
12	
1	
2	
3	
4	
5	
6	
7	
8	
9	
10	
11	

POWER-HOUR-INTENTIONS:

_____

_____

_____

_____

_____

_____

_____

TODAYS WINS:

_____

_____

_____

_____

_____

INTENTIONAL LEARNING:

_____

_____

_____

_____

_____

_____

TIME	PM PLAN
12	
1	
2	
3	
4	
5	
6	
7	
8	
9	
10	
11	

DATE: _____

TODAY'S GOALS:

_____

_____

_____

_____

_____

MUST DO LIST:

_____

_____

_____

_____

_____

_____

_____

NOTES:

TIME	AM PLAN
12	
1	
2	
3	
4	
5	
6	
7	
8	
9	
10	
11	

_____

_____

_____

_____

_____

_____

_____

POWER-HOUR-INTENTIONS:

_____
_____
_____
_____
_____
_____
_____

TODAYS WINS:

_____
_____
_____
_____
_____
_____

INTENTIONAL LEARNING:

_____
_____
_____
_____
_____
_____

TIME	PM PLAN
12	
1	
2	
3	
4	
5	
6	
7	
8	
9	
10	
11	

DATE: _____

TODAY'S GOALS:

_____
_____
_____
_____
_____

MUST DO LIST:

_____
_____
_____
_____
_____
_____
_____

NOTES:

TIME	AM PLAN
12	
1	
2	
3	
4	
5	
6	
7	
8	
9	
10	
11	

_____
_____
_____
_____
_____
_____
_____

POWER-HOUR-INTENTIONS:

_____

_____

_____

_____

_____

_____

TODAYS WINS:

_____

_____

_____

_____

_____

_____

INTENTIONAL LEARNING:

_____

_____

_____

_____

_____

_____

____

TIME	PM PLAN
12	
1	
2	
3	
4	
5	
6	
7	
8	
9	
10	
11	

DATE: _____

TODAY'S GOALS:

_____
_____
_____
_____
_____

MUST DO LIST:

_____
_____
_____
_____
_____
_____
_____
_____

NOTES:

TIME	AM PLAN
12	
1	
2	
3	
4	
5	
6	
7	
8	
9	
10	
11	

_____
_____
_____
_____
_____
_____
_____

POWER-HOUR-INTENTIONS:

_____
_____
_____
_____
_____
_____

TODAYS WINS:

_____
_____
_____
_____
_____
_____

INTENTIONAL LEARNING:

_____
_____
_____
_____
_____
_____
_____

TIME	PM PLAN
12	
1	
2	
3	
4	
5	
6	
7	
8	
9	
10	
11	

DATE: _____

TODAY'S GOALS:

_____
_____
_____
_____
_____

MUST DO LIST:

_____
_____
_____
_____
_____
_____
_____

NOTES:

TIME	AM PLAN
12	
1	
2	
3	
4	
5	
6	
7	
8	
9	
10	
11	

_____
_____
_____
_____
_____
_____
_____

POWER-HOUR-INTENTIONS:

_____
_____
_____
_____
_____
_____

TODAYS WINS:

_____
_____
_____
_____
_____
_____

INTENTIONAL LEARNING:

_____
_____
_____
_____
_____
_____

TIME	PM PLAN
12	
1	
2	
3	
4	
5	
6	
7	
8	
9	
10	
11	

DATE: _____

TODAY'S GOALS:

_____
_____
_____
_____
_____

MUST DO LIST:

_____
_____
_____
_____
_____
_____
_____

NOTES:

TIME	AM PLAN
12	
1	
2	
3	
4	
5	
6	
7	
8	
9	
10	
11	

_____
_____
_____
_____
_____
_____
_____

POWER-HOUR-INTENTIONS:

_____
_____
_____
_____
_____
_____

TODAYS WINS:

_____
_____
_____
_____
_____

INTENTIONAL LEARNING:

_____
_____
_____
_____
_____
_____

TIME	PM PLAN
12	
1	
2	
3	
4	
5	
6	
7	
8	
9	
10	
11	

DATE: _____

TODAY'S GOALS:

_____
_____
_____
_____
_____
_____

MUST DO LIST:

_____
_____
_____
_____
_____
_____
_____

NOTES:

_____
_____
_____
_____
_____
_____
_____

TIME	AM PLAN
12	
1	
2	
3	
4	
5	
6	
7	
8	
9	
10	
11	

POWER-HOUR-INTENTIONS:

_____
_____
_____
_____
_____
_____

TODAYS WINS:

_____
_____
_____
_____
_____
_____

INTENTIONAL LEARNING:

_____
_____
_____
_____
_____
_____

TIME	PM PLAN
12	
1	
2	
3	
4	
5	
6	
7	
8	
9	
10	
11	

DATE: _____

TODAY'S GOALS:

_____
_____
_____
_____
_____
_____

MUST DO LIST:

_____
_____
_____
_____
_____
_____
_____

NOTES:

_____
_____
_____
_____
_____
_____
_____

TIME	AM PLAN
12	
1	
2	
3	
4	
5	
6	
7	
8	
9	
10	
11	

POWER-HOUR-INTENTIONS:

_____
_____
_____
_____
_____
_____

TODAYS WINS:

_____
_____
_____
_____
_____
_____

INTENTIONAL LEARNING:

_____
_____
_____
_____
_____
_____

TIME	PM PLAN
12	
1	
2	
3	
4	
5	
6	
7	
8	
9	
10	
11	

DATE: _____

TODAY'S GOALS:

_____
_____
_____
_____
_____

MUST DO LIST:

_____
_____
_____
_____
_____
_____
_____

NOTES:

_____
_____
_____
_____
_____
_____
_____

TIME	AM PLAN
12	
1	
2	
3	
4	
5	
6	
7	
8	
9	
10	
11	

POWER-HOUR-INTENTIONS:

_____
_____
_____
_____
_____
_____

TODAYS WINS:

_____
_____
_____
_____
_____

INTENTIONAL LEARNING:

_____
_____
_____
_____
_____
_____

TIME	PM PLAN
12	
1	
2	
3	
4	
5	
6	
7	
8	
9	
10	
11	

DATE: _____

TODAY'S GOALS:

_____
_____
_____
_____
_____

MUST DO LIST:

_____
_____
_____
_____
_____
_____
_____

NOTES:

TIME	AM PLAN
12	
1	
2	
3	
4	
5	
6	
7	
8	
9	
10	
11	

_____
_____
_____
_____
_____
_____
_____

POWER-HOUR-INTENTIONS:

_____

_____

_____

_____

_____

_____

TODAYS WINS:

_____

_____

_____

_____

_____

_____

INTENTIONAL LEARNING:

_____

_____

_____

_____

_____

_____

_____

TIME	PM PLAN
12	
1	
2	
3	
4	
5	
6	
7	
8	
9	
10	
11	

DATE: _____

TODAY'S GOALS:

_____
_____
_____
_____
_____

MUST DO LIST:

_____
_____
_____
_____
_____
_____

NOTES:

TIME	AM PLAN
12	
1	
2	
3	
4	
5	
6	
7	
8	
9	
10	
11	

_____
_____
_____
_____
_____
_____
_____

POWER-HOUR-INTENTIONS:

_____

_____

_____

_____

_____

TODAYS WINS:

_____

_____

_____

_____

_____

INTENTIONAL LEARNING:

_____

_____

_____

_____

_____

_____

TIME	PM PLAN
12	
1	
2	
3	
4	
5	
6	
7	
8	
9	
10	
11	

DATE: _____

TODAY'S GOALS:

_____
_____
_____
_____
_____

MUST DO LIST:

_____
_____
_____
_____
_____
_____
_____

NOTES:

TIME	AM PLAN
12	
1	
2	
3	
4	
5	
6	
7	
8	
9	
10	
11	

_____
_____
_____
_____
_____
_____
_____

POWER-HOUR-INTENTIONS:

_____

_____

_____

_____

_____

_____

TODAYS WINS:

_____

_____

_____

_____

_____

INTENTIONAL LEARNING:

_____

_____

_____

_____

_____

_____

_____

TIME	PM PLAN
12	
1	
2	
3	
4	
5	
6	
7	
8	
9	
10	
11	

DATE: _____

TODAY'S GOALS:

_____
_____
_____
_____
_____

MUST DO LIST:

_____
_____
_____
_____
_____
_____

NOTES:

TIME	AM PLAN
12	
1	
2	
3	
4	
5	
6	
7	
8	
9	
10	
11	

_____
_____
_____
_____
_____
_____
_____

POWER-HOUR-INTENTIONS:

_____

_____

_____

_____

_____

_____

TODAYS WINS:

_____

_____

_____

_____

_____

_____

INTENTIONAL LEARNING:

_____

_____

_____

_____

_____

_____

TIME	PM PLAN
12	
1	
2	
3	
4	
5	
6	
7	
8	
9	
10	
11	

DATE: _____

TODAY'S GOALS:

_____
_____
_____
_____
_____

MUST DO LIST:

_____
_____
_____
_____
_____
_____
_____

NOTES:

TIME	AM PLAN
12	
1	
2	
3	
4	
5	
6	
7	
8	
9	
10	
11	

_____
_____
_____
_____
_____
_____
_____

POWER-HOUR-INTENTIONS:

_____
_____
_____
_____
_____
_____

TODAYS WINS:

_____
_____
_____
_____
_____
_____
_____

INTENTIONAL LEARNING:

_____
_____
_____
_____
_____
_____
_____
_____

TIME	PM PLAN
12	
1	
2	
3	
4	
5	
6	
7	
8	
9	
10	
11	

DATE: _____

TODAY'S GOALS:

_____
_____
_____
_____
_____

MUST DO LIST:

_____
_____
_____
_____
_____
_____
_____

NOTES:

TIME	AM PLAN
12	
1	
2	
3	
4	
5	
6	
7	
8	
9	
10	
11	

_____
_____
_____
_____
_____
_____

POWER-HOUR-INTENTIONS:

_____
_____
_____
_____
_____
_____

TODAYS WINS:

_____
_____
_____
_____
_____
_____

INTENTIONAL LEARNING:

_____
_____
_____
_____
_____
_____
_____

TIME	PM PLAN
12	
1	
2	
3	
4	
5	
6	
7	
8	
9	
10	
11	

DATE: _____

TODAY'S GOALS:

_____
_____
_____
_____
_____
_____

MUST DO LIST:

_____
_____
_____
_____
_____
_____
_____

NOTES:

TIME	AM PLAN
12	
1	
2	
3	
4	
5	
6	
7	
8	
9	
10	
11	

_____
_____
_____
_____
_____
_____
_____

POWER-HOUR-INTENTIONS:

_____
_____
_____
_____
_____
_____

TODAYS WINS:

_____
_____
_____
_____
_____
_____
_____

INTENTIONAL LEARNING:

_____
_____
_____
_____
_____
_____
_____

TIME	PM PLAN
12	
1	
2	
3	
4	
5	
6	
7	
8	
9	
10	
11	

DATE: _____

TODAY'S GOALS:

_____
_____
_____
_____
_____

MUST DO LIST:

_____
_____
_____
_____
_____
_____
_____

NOTES:

TIME	AM PLAN
12	
1	
2	
3	
4	
5	
6	
7	
8	
9	
10	
11	

_____
_____
_____
_____
_____
_____
_____

POWER-HOUR-INTENTIONS:

_____

_____

_____

_____

_____

_____

TODAYS WINS:

_____

_____

_____

_____

_____

_____

_____

INTENTIONAL LEARNING:

_____

_____

_____

_____

_____

_____

_____

TIME	PM PLAN
12	
1	
2	
3	
4	
5	
6	
7	
8	
9	
10	
11	

DATE: _____

TODAY'S GOALS:

_____
_____
_____
_____
_____

MUST DO LIST:

_____
_____
_____
_____
_____
_____
_____

NOTES:

TIME	AM PLAN
12	
1	
2	
3	
4	
5	
6	
7	
8	
9	
10	
11	

_____
_____
_____
_____
_____
_____
_____

POWER-HOUR-INTENTIONS:

_____

_____

_____

_____

_____

_____

TODAYS WINS:

_____

_____

_____

_____

_____

INTENTIONAL LEARNING:

_____

_____

_____

_____

_____

_____

TIME	PM PLAN
12	
1	
2	
3	
4	
5	
6	
7	
8	
9	
10	
11	

DATE: _____

TODAY'S GOALS:

_____
_____
_____
_____

MUST DO LIST:

_____
_____
_____
_____
_____
_____

NOTES:

TIME	AM PLAN
12	
1	
2	
3	
4	
5	
6	
7	
8	
9	
10	
11	

_____
_____
_____
_____
_____
_____
_____
_____

POWER-HOUR-INTENTIONS:

_____
_____
_____
_____
_____
_____

TODAYS WINS:

TIME	PM PLAN
12	
1	
2	
3	
4	
5	
6	
7	
8	
9	
10	
11	

INTENTIONAL LEARNING:

DATE: _____

TODAY'S GOALS:

_____
_____
_____
_____
_____

MUST DO LIST:

_____
_____
_____
_____
_____
_____
_____

NOTES:

TIME	AM PLAN
12	
1	
2	
3	
4	
5	
6	
7	
8	
9	
10	
11	

_____
_____
_____
_____
_____
_____
_____

POWER-HOUR-INTENTIONS:

_____

_____

_____

_____

_____

TODAYS WINS:

_____

_____

_____

_____

_____

INTENTIONAL LEARNING:

_____

_____

_____

_____

_____

_____

TIME	PM PLAN
12	
1	
2	
3	
4	
5	
6	
7	
8	
9	
10	
11	

DATE: _____

TODAY'S GOALS:

_____
_____
_____
_____
_____

MUST DO LIST:

_____
_____
_____
_____
_____
_____
_____

NOTES:

TIME	AM PLAN
12	
1	
2	
3	
4	
5	
6	
7	
8	
9	
10	
11	

_____
_____
_____
_____
_____
_____
_____
_____

POWER-HOUR-INTENTIONS:

_____
_____
_____
_____
_____
_____

TODAYS WINS:

_____
_____
_____
_____
_____
_____

INTENTIONAL LEARNING:

_____
_____
_____
_____
_____
_____
_____
_____

TIME	PM PLAN
12	
1	
2	
3	
4	
5	
6	
7	
8	
9	
10	
11	

DATE: _____

TODAY'S GOALS:

_____
_____
_____
_____
_____

MUST DO LIST:

_____
_____
_____
_____
_____
_____
_____

NOTES:

TIME	AM PLAN
12	
1	
2	
3	
4	
5	
6	
7	
8	
9	
10	
11	

_____
_____
_____
_____
_____
_____
_____

POWER-HOUR-INTENTIONS:

_____
_____
_____
_____
_____
_____

TODAYS WINS:

_____
_____
_____
_____
_____
_____

INTENTIONAL LEARNING:

_____
_____
_____
_____
_____
_____
_____

TIME	PM PLAN
12	
1	
2	
3	
4	
5	
6	
7	
8	
9	
10	
11	

DATE: _____

TODAY'S GOALS:

_____
_____
_____
_____
_____

MUST DO LIST:

_____
_____
_____
_____
_____
_____

NOTES:

TIME	AM PLAN
12	
1	
2	
3	
4	
5	
6	
7	
8	
9	
10	
11	

_____
_____
_____
_____
_____
_____
_____

POWER-HOUR-INTENTIONS:

_____

_____

_____

_____

_____

_____

TODAYS WINS:

_____

_____

_____

_____

_____

_____

INTENTIONAL LEARNING:

_____

_____

_____

_____

_____

_____

_____

TIME	PM PLAN
12	
1	
2	
3	
4	
5	
6	
7	
8	
9	
10	
11	

DATE: _____

TODAY'S GOALS:

_____
_____
_____
_____
_____

MUST DO LIST:

_____
_____
_____
_____
_____
_____
_____

NOTES:

TIME	AM PLAN
12	
1	
2	
3	
4	
5	
6	
7	
8	
9	
10	
11	

_____
_____
_____
_____
_____
_____
_____

POWER-HOUR-INTENTIONS:

_____
_____
_____
_____
_____
_____

TODAYS WINS:

_____
_____
_____
_____
_____

INTENTIONAL LEARNING:

_____
_____
_____
_____
_____
_____

TIME	PM PLAN
12	
1	
2	
3	
4	
5	
6	
7	
8	
9	
10	
11	

DATE: _____

TODAY'S GOALS:

_____
_____
_____
_____
_____

MUST DO LIST:

_____
_____
_____
_____
_____
_____

NOTES:

TIME	AM PLAN
12	
1	
2	
3	
4	
5	
6	
7	
8	
9	
10	
11	

_____
_____
_____
_____
_____
_____
_____

POWER-HOUR-INTENTIONS:

_____

_____

_____

_____

_____

_____

TODAYS WINS:

_____

_____

_____

_____

_____

_____

INTENTIONAL LEARNING:

_____

_____

_____

_____

_____

_____

_____

TIME	PM PLAN
12	
1	
2	
3	
4	
5	
6	
7	
8	
9	
10	
11	

DATE: _____

TODAY'S GOALS:

_____
_____
_____
_____
_____

MUST DO LIST:

_____
_____
_____
_____
_____
_____
_____

NOTES:

TIME	AM PLAN
12	
1	
2	
3	
4	
5	
6	
7	
8	
9	
10	
11	

_____
_____
_____
_____
_____
_____
_____

POWER-HOUR-INTENTIONS:

_____

_____

_____

_____

_____

_____

TODAYS WINS:

_____

_____

_____

_____

_____

_____

INTENTIONAL LEARNING:

_____

_____

_____

_____

_____

_____

_____

TIME	PM PLAN
12	
1	
2	
3	
4	
5	
6	
7	
8	
9	
10	
11	

DATE: _____

TODAY'S GOALS:

_____

_____

_____

_____

MUST DO LIST:

_____

_____

_____

_____

_____

_____

NOTES:

TIME	AM PLAN
12	
1	
2	
3	
4	
5	
6	
7	
8	
9	
10	
11	

_____

_____

_____

_____

_____

_____

_____

POWER-HOUR-INTENTIONS:

_____
_____
_____
_____
_____
_____

TODAYS WINS:

_____
_____
_____
_____
_____
_____

INTENTIONAL LEARNING:

_____
_____
_____
_____
_____
_____
_____

TIME	PM PLAN
12	
1	
2	
3	
4	
5	
6	
7	
8	
9	
10	
11	

DATE: _____

TODAY'S GOALS:

_____
_____
_____
_____
_____

MUST DO LIST:

_____
_____
_____
_____
_____
_____
_____

NOTES:

TIME	AM PLAN
12	
1	
2	
3	
4	
5	
6	
7	
8	
9	
10	
11	

_____
_____
_____
_____
_____
_____
_____

POWER-HOUR-INTENTIONS:

_____
_____
_____
_____
_____
_____

TODAYS WINS:

_____
_____
_____
_____
_____
_____

INTENTIONAL LEARNING:

_____
_____
_____
_____
_____
_____
_____

TIME	PM PLAN
12	
1	
2	
3	
4	
5	
6	
7	
8	
9	
10	
11	

DATE: _____

TODAY'S GOALS:

_____
_____
_____
_____

MUST DO LIST:

_____
_____
_____
_____
_____
_____

NOTES:

TIME	AM PLAN
12	
1	
2	
3	
4	
5	
6	
7	
8	
9	
10	
11	

_____
_____
_____
_____
_____
_____
_____

POWER-HOUR-INTENTIONS:

_____

_____

_____

_____

_____

_____

TODAYS WINS:

_____

_____

_____

_____

_____

_____

INTENTIONAL LEARNING:

_____

_____

_____

_____

_____

_____

_____

_____

TIME	PM PLAN
12	
1	
2	
3	
4	
5	
6	
7	
8	
9	
10	
11	

DATE: _____

TODAY'S GOALS:

_____
_____
_____
_____
_____

MUST DO LIST:

_____
_____
_____
_____
_____
_____
_____

NOTES:

TIME	AM PLAN
12	
1	
2	
3	
4	
5	
6	
7	
8	
9	
10	
11	

_____
_____
_____
_____
_____
_____
_____

POWER-HOUR-INTENTIONS:

_____

_____

_____

_____

_____

TODAYS WINS:

_____

_____

_____

_____

_____

_____

INTENTIONAL LEARNING:

_____

_____

_____

_____

_____

_____

_____

TIME	PM PLAN
12	
1	
2	
3	
4	
5	
6	
7	
8	
9	
10	
11	

DATE: _____

TODAY'S GOALS:

_____
_____
_____
_____
_____

MUST DO LIST:

_____
_____
_____
_____
_____
_____
_____

NOTES:

TIME	AM PLAN
12	
1	
2	
3	
4	
5	
6	
7	
8	
9	
10	
11	

_____
_____
_____
_____
_____
_____
_____

POWER-HOUR-INTENTIONS:

_____

_____

_____

_____

_____

_____

TODAYS WINS:

_____

_____

_____

_____

_____

INTENTIONAL LEARNING:

_____

_____

_____

_____

_____

_____

_____

TIME	PM PLAN
12	
1	
2	
3	
4	
5	
6	
7	
8	
9	
10	
11	

DATE: _____

TODAY'S GOALS:

_____
_____
_____
_____

MUST DO LIST:

_____
_____
_____
_____
_____
_____

NOTES:

TIME	AM PLAN
12	
1	
2	
3	
4	
5	
6	
7	
8	
9	
10	
11	

_____
_____
_____
_____
_____
_____
_____
_____

POWER-HOUR-INTENTIONS:

_____

_____

_____

_____

_____

_____

TODAYS WINS:

_____

_____

_____

_____

_____

INTENTIONAL LEARNING:

_____

_____

_____

_____

_____

_____

TIME	PM PLAN
12	
1	
2	
3	
4	
5	
6	
7	
8	
9	
10	
11	

DATE: _____

TODAY'S GOALS:

_____
_____
_____
_____
_____

MUST DO LIST:

_____
_____
_____
_____
_____
_____
_____

NOTES:

TIME	AM PLAN
12	
1	
2	
3	
4	
5	
6	
7	
8	
9	
10	
11	

_____
_____
_____
_____
_____
_____
_____

POWER-HOUR-INTENTIONS:

_____

_____

_____

_____

_____

_____

TODAYS WINS:

_____

_____

_____

_____

_____

_____

INTENTIONAL LEARNING:

_____

_____

_____

_____

_____

_____

_____

TIME	PM PLAN
12	
1	
2	
3	
4	
5	
6	
7	
8	
9	
10	
11	

DATE: _____

TODAY'S GOALS:

_____

_____

_____

_____

MUST DO LIST:

_____

_____

_____

_____

_____

_____

_____

NOTES:

TIME	AM PLAN
12	
1	
2	
3	
4	
5	
6	
7	
8	
9	
10	
11	

_____

_____

_____

_____

_____

_____

POWER-HOUR-INTENTIONS:

_____

_____

_____

_____

_____

TODAYS WINS:

_____

_____

_____

_____

_____

INTENTIONAL LEARNING:

_____

_____

_____

_____

_____

_____

_____

TIME	PM PLAN
12	
1	
2	
3	
4	
5	
6	
7	
8	
9	
10	
11	

DATE: _____

TODAY'S GOALS:

_____
_____
_____
_____

MUST DO LIST:

_____
_____
_____
_____
_____
_____

NOTES:

TIME	AM PLAN
12	
1	
2	
3	
4	
5	
6	
7	
8	
9	
10	
11	

_____
_____
_____
_____
_____
_____
_____

POWER-HOUR-INTENTIONS:

_____

_____

_____

_____

_____

_____

TODAYS WINS:

_____

_____

_____

_____

_____

_____

INTENTIONAL LEARNING:

_____

_____

_____

_____

_____

_____

_____

TIME	PM PLAN
12	
1	
2	
3	
4	
5	
6	
7	
8	
9	
10	
11	

DATE: _____

TODAY'S GOALS:

_____
_____
_____
_____
_____
_____

MUST DO LIST:

_____
_____
_____
_____
_____
_____
_____

NOTES:

TIME	AM PLAN
12	
1	
2	
3	
4	
5	
6	
7	
8	
9	
10	
11	

_____
_____
_____
_____
_____
_____
_____

POWER-HOUR-INTENTIONS:

_____

_____

_____

_____

_____

TODAYS WINS:

_____

_____

_____

_____

_____

INTENTIONAL LEARNING:

_____

_____

_____

_____

_____

_____

TIME	PM PLAN
12	
1	
2	
3	
4	
5	
6	
7	
8	
9	
10	
11	

DATE: _____

TODAY'S GOALS:

_____
_____
_____
_____

MUST DO LIST:

_____
_____
_____
_____
_____
_____
_____

NOTES:

TIME	AM PLAN
12	
1	
2	
3	
4	
5	
6	
7	
8	
9	
10	
11	

_____
_____
_____
_____
_____
_____
_____
_____

POWER-HOUR-INTENTIONS:

_____

_____

_____

_____

_____

_____

TODAYS WINS:

_____

_____

_____

_____

_____

INTENTIONAL LEARNING:

_____

_____

_____

_____

_____

_____

TIME	PM PLAN
12	
1	
2	
3	
4	
5	
6	
7	
8	
9	
10	
11	

DATE: _____

TODAY'S GOALS:

_____

_____

_____

_____

_____

MUST DO LIST:

_____

_____

_____

_____

_____

_____

_____

NOTES:

TIME	AM PLAN
12	
1	
2	
3	
4	
5	
6	
7	
8	
9	
10	
11	

_____

_____

_____

_____

_____

_____

_____

POWER-HOUR-INTENTIONS:

_____

_____

_____

_____

_____

TODAYS WINS:

_____

_____

_____

_____

_____

_____

INTENTIONAL LEARNING:

_____

_____

_____

_____

_____

_____

_____

TIME	PM PLAN
12	
1	
2	
3	
4	
5	
6	
7	
8	
9	
10	
11	

DATE: _____

TODAY'S GOALS:

_____
_____
_____
_____
_____

MUST DO LIST:

_____
_____
_____
_____
_____
_____
_____

NOTES:

TIME	AM PLAN
12	
1	
2	
3	
4	
5	
6	
7	
8	
9	
10	
11	

_____
_____
_____
_____
_____
_____
_____

POWER-HOUR-INTENTIONS:

_____
_____
_____
_____
_____
_____

TODAYS WINS:

_____
_____
_____
_____
_____
_____

INTENTIONAL LEARNING:

_____
_____
_____
_____
_____
_____
_____

TIME	PM PLAN
12	
1	
2	
3	
4	
5	
6	
7	
8	
9	
10	
11	

DATE: _____

TODAY'S GOALS:

_____
_____
_____
_____
_____

MUST DO LIST:

_____
_____
_____
_____
_____
_____
_____

NOTES:

TIME	AM PLAN
12	
1	
2	
3	
4	
5	
6	
7	
8	
9	
10	
11	

_____
_____
_____
_____
_____
_____
_____

POWER-HOUR-INTENTIONS:

_____
_____
_____
_____
_____
_____

TODAYS WINS:

_____
_____
_____
_____
_____

INTENTIONAL LEARNING:

_____
_____
_____
_____
_____
_____

TIME	PM PLAN
12	
1	
2	
3	
4	
5	
6	
7	
8	
9	
10	
11	

DATE: _____

TODAY'S GOALS:

_____
_____
_____
_____
_____

MUST DO LIST:

_____
_____
_____
_____
_____
_____
_____

NOTES:

TIME	AM PLAN
12	
1	
2	
3	
4	
5	
6	
7	
8	
9	
10	
11	

_____
_____
_____
_____
_____
_____
_____

POWER-HOUR-INTENTIONS:

_____
_____
_____
_____
_____
_____

TODAYS WINS:

_____
_____
_____
_____
_____

INTENTIONAL LEARNING:

_____
_____
_____
_____
_____
_____

TIME	PM PLAN
12	
1	
2	
3	
4	
5	
6	
7	
8	
9	
10	
11	

DATE: _____

TODAY'S GOALS:

_____
_____
_____
_____
_____

MUST DO LIST:

_____
_____
_____
_____
_____
_____
_____

NOTES:

TIME	AM PLAN
12	
1	
2	
3	
4	
5	
6	
7	
8	
9	
10	
11	

_____
_____
_____
_____
_____
_____
_____

POWER-HOUR-INTENTIONS:

_____

_____

_____

_____

_____

_____

TODAYS WINS:

_____

_____

_____

_____

_____

INTENTIONAL LEARNING:

_____

_____

_____

_____

_____

_____

_____

TIME	PM PLAN
12	
1	
2	
3	
4	
5	
6	
7	
8	
9	
10	
11	

DATE: _____

TODAY'S GOALS:

_____

_____

_____

_____

_____

MUST DO LIST:

_____

_____

_____

_____

_____

_____

_____

TIME	AM PLAN
12	
1	
2	
3	
4	
5	
6	
7	
8	
9	
10	
11	

NOTES:

_____

_____

_____

_____

_____

_____

_____

POWER-HOUR-INTENTIONS:

_____
_____
_____
_____
_____
_____

TODAYS WINS:

_____
_____
_____
_____
_____

INTENTIONAL LEARNING:

_____
_____
_____
_____
_____
_____

TIME	PM PLAN
12	
1	
2	
3	
4	
5	
6	
7	
8	
9	
10	
11	

DATE: _____

TODAY'S GOALS:

_____
_____
_____
_____
_____

MUST DO LIST:

_____
_____
_____
_____
_____
_____
_____

NOTES:

TIME	AM PLAN
12	
1	
2	
3	
4	
5	
6	
7	
8	
9	
10	
11	

_____
_____
_____
_____
_____
_____
_____

POWER-HOUR-INTENTIONS:

_____

_____

_____

_____

_____

_____

TODAYS WINS:

_____

_____

_____

_____

_____

_____

INTENTIONAL LEARNING:

_____

_____

_____

_____

_____

_____

_____

TIME	PM PLAN
12	
1	
2	
3	
4	
5	
6	
7	
8	
9	
10	
11	

DATE: _____

TODAY'S GOALS:

_____
_____
_____
_____
_____

MUST DO LIST:

_____
_____
_____
_____
_____
_____
_____

NOTES:

TIME	AM PLAN
12	
1	
2	
3	
4	
5	
6	
7	
8	
9	
10	
11	

_____
_____
_____
_____
_____
_____
_____

POWER-HOUR-INTENTIONS:

_____
_____
_____
_____
_____
_____

TODAYS WINS:

_____
_____
_____
_____
_____
_____

INTENTIONAL LEARNING:

_____
_____
_____
_____
_____
_____
_____

TIME	PM PLAN
12	
1	
2	
3	
4	
5	
6	
7	
8	
9	
10	
11	

DATE: _____

TODAY'S GOALS:

_____

_____

_____

_____

MUST DO LIST:

_____

_____

_____

_____

_____

_____

_____

NOTES:

TIME	AM PLAN
12	
1	
2	
3	
4	
5	
6	
7	
8	
9	
10	
11	

_____

_____

_____

_____

_____

_____

_____

POWER-HOUR-INTENTIONS:

_____

_____

_____

_____

_____

_____

TODAYS WINS:

TIME	PM PLAN
12	
1	
2	
3	
4	
5	
6	
7	
8	
9	
10	
11	

INTENTIONAL LEARNING:

DATE: _____

TODAY'S GOALS:

_____
_____
_____
_____
_____

MUST DO LIST:

_____
_____
_____
_____
_____
_____
_____

NOTES:

TIME	AM PLAN
12	
1	
2	
3	
4	
5	
6	
7	
8	
9	
10	
11	

_____
_____
_____
_____
_____
_____
_____
_____

POWER-HOUR-INTENTIONS:

_____

_____

_____

_____

_____

_____

TODAYS WINS:

_____

_____

_____

_____

_____

INTENTIONAL LEARNING:

_____

_____

_____

_____

_____

_____

TIME	PM PLAN
12	
1	
2	
3	
4	
5	
6	
7	
8	
9	
10	
11	

DATE: _____

TODAY'S GOALS:

_____
_____
_____
_____
_____

MUST DO LIST:

_____
_____
_____
_____
_____
_____
_____

NOTES:

TIME	AM PLAN
12	
1	
2	
3	
4	
5	
6	
7	
8	
9	
10	
11	

_____
_____
_____
_____
_____
_____
_____
_____

POWER-HOUR-INTENTIONS:

_____
_____
_____
_____
_____
_____

TODAYS WINS:

_____
_____
_____
_____
_____
_____

INTENTIONAL LEARNING:

_____
_____
_____
_____
_____
_____
_____
_____

TIME	PM PLAN
12	
1	
2	
3	
4	
5	
6	
7	
8	
9	
10	
11	

DATE: _____

TODAY'S GOALS:

_____
_____
_____
_____
_____

MUST DO LIST:

_____
_____
_____
_____
_____
_____
_____

NOTES:

TIME	AM PLAN
12	
1	
2	
3	
4	
5	
6	
7	
8	
9	
10	
11	

_____
_____
_____
_____
_____
_____
_____

POWER-HOUR-INTENTIONS:

_____

_____

_____

_____

_____

_____

TODAYS WINS:

_____

_____

_____

_____

_____

INTENTIONAL LEARNING:

_____

_____

_____

_____

_____

_____

TIME	PM PLAN
12	
1	
2	
3	
4	
5	
6	
7	
8	
9	
10	
11	

DATE: _____

TODAY'S GOALS:

_____
_____
_____
_____
_____

MUST DO LIST:

_____
_____
_____
_____
_____
_____
_____
_____

NOTES:

TIME	AM PLAN
12	
1	
2	
3	
4	
5	
6	
7	
8	
9	
10	
11	

_____
_____
_____
_____
_____
_____
_____

POWER-HOUR-INTENTIONS:

_____
_____
_____
_____
_____
_____

TODAYS WINS:

_____

_____

_____

_____

_____

_____

INTENTIONAL LEARNING:

_____

_____

_____

_____

_____

_____

_____

TIME	PM PLAN
12	
1	
2	
3	
4	
5	
6	
7	
8	
9	
10	
11	

DATE: _____

TODAY'S GOALS:

_____
_____
_____
_____

MUST DO LIST:

_____
_____
_____
_____
_____
_____
_____

NOTES:

TIME	AM PLAN
12	
1	
2	
3	
4	
5	
6	
7	
8	
9	
10	
11	

_____
_____
_____
_____
_____
_____
_____

POWER-HOUR-INTENTIONS:

_____

_____

_____

_____

_____

_____

TODAYS WINS:

TIME	PM PLAN
12	
1	
2	
3	
4	
5	
6	
7	
8	
9	
10	
11	

INTENTIONAL LEARNING:

DATE: _____

TODAY'S GOALS:

_____
_____
_____
_____
_____

MUST DO LIST:

_____
_____
_____
_____
_____
_____
_____

NOTES:

TIME	AM PLAN
12	
1	
2	
3	
4	
5	
6	
7	
8	
9	
10	
11	

_____
_____
_____
_____
_____
_____
_____
_____

POWER-HOUR-INTENTIONS:

_____
_____
_____
_____
_____
_____

TODAYS WINS:

_____
_____
_____
_____
_____
_____
_____

INTENTIONAL LEARNING:

_____
_____
_____
_____
_____
_____
_____
_____

TIME	PM PLAN
12	
1	
2	
3	
4	
5	
6	
7	
8	
9	
10	
11	

DATE: _____

TODAY'S GOALS:

_____
_____
_____
_____
_____

MUST DO LIST:

_____
_____
_____
_____
_____
_____
_____

NOTES:

TIME	AM PLAN
12	
1	
2	
3	
4	
5	
6	
7	
8	
9	
10	
11	

_____
_____
_____
_____
_____
_____
_____

POWER-HOUR-INTENTIONS:

_____

_____

_____

_____

_____

_____

TODAYS WINS:

_____

_____

_____

_____

_____

INTENTIONAL LEARNING:

_____

_____

_____

_____

_____

_____

TIME	PM PLAN
12	
1	
2	
3	
4	
5	
6	
7	
8	
9	
10	
11	

DATE: _____

TODAY'S GOALS:

_____
_____
_____
_____
_____

MUST DO LIST:

_____
_____
_____
_____
_____
_____
_____

NOTES:

_____
_____
_____
_____
_____
_____
_____

TIME	AM PLAN
12	
1	
2	
3	
4	
5	
6	
7	
8	
9	
10	
11	

POWER-HOUR-INTENTIONS:

_____

_____

_____

_____

_____

TODAYS WINS:

_____

_____

_____

_____

_____

_____

INTENTIONAL LEARNING:

_____

_____

_____

_____

_____

_____

_____

TIME	PM PLAN
12	
1	
2	
3	
4	
5	
6	
7	
8	
9	
10	
11	

DATE: _____

TODAY'S GOALS:

_____
_____
_____
_____
_____

MUST DO LIST:

_____
_____
_____
_____
_____
_____

NOTES:

TIME	AM PLAN
12	
1	
2	
3	
4	
5	
6	
7	
8	
9	
10	
11	

_____
_____
_____
_____
_____
_____
_____

POWER-HOUR-INTENTIONS:

_____

_____

_____

_____

_____

_____

TODAYS WINS:

TIME	PM PLAN
12	
1	
2	
3	
4	
5	
6	
7	
8	
9	
10	
11	

INTENTIONAL LEARNING:

DATE: _____

TODAY'S GOALS:

_____
_____
_____
_____
_____

MUST DO LIST:

_____
_____
_____
_____
_____
_____
_____

NOTES:

TIME	AM PLAN
12	
1	
2	
3	
4	
5	
6	
7	
8	
9	
10	
11	

_____
_____
_____
_____
_____
_____

POWER-HOUR-INTENTIONS:

_____
_____
_____
_____
_____
_____

TODAYS WINS:

_____
_____
_____
_____
_____
_____

INTENTIONAL LEARNING:

_____
_____
_____
_____
_____
_____
_____

TIME	PM PLAN
12	
1	
2	
3	
4	
5	
6	
7	
8	
9	
10	
11	

DATE: _____

TODAY'S GOALS:

_____
_____
_____
_____
_____

MUST DO LIST:

_____
_____
_____
_____
_____
_____
_____

NOTES:

_____
_____
_____
_____
_____
_____
_____

TIME	AM PLAN
12	
1	
2	
3	
4	
5	
6	
7	
8	
9	
10	
11	

POWER-HOUR-INTENTIONS:

_____
_____
_____
_____
_____
_____

TODAYS WINS:

_____
_____
_____
_____
_____
_____

INTENTIONAL LEARNING:

_____
_____
_____
_____
_____
_____
_____

TIME	PM PLAN
12	
1	
2	
3	
4	
5	
6	
7	
8	
9	
10	
11	

DATE: _____

TODAY'S GOALS:

_____
_____
_____
_____
_____

MUST DO LIST:

_____
_____
_____
_____
_____
_____
_____

NOTES:

TIME	AM PLAN
12	
1	
2	
3	
4	
5	
6	
7	
8	
9	
10	
11	

_____
_____
_____
_____
_____
_____
_____

POWER-HOUR-INTENTIONS:

_____

_____

_____

_____

_____

_____

TODAYS WINS:

_____

_____

_____

_____

_____

_____

INTENTIONAL LEARNING:

_____

_____

_____

_____

_____

_____

_____

TIME	PM PLAN
12	
1	
2	
3	
4	
5	
6	
7	
8	
9	
10	
11	

DATE: _____

TODAY'S GOALS:

_____
_____
_____
_____

MUST DO LIST:

_____
_____
_____
_____
_____
_____
_____

NOTES:

TIME	AM PLAN
12	
1	
2	
3	
4	
5	
6	
7	
8	
9	
10	
11	

_____
_____
_____
_____
_____
_____
_____

POWER-HOUR-INTENTIONS:

_____
_____
_____
_____
_____
_____

TODAYS WINS:

_____
_____
_____
_____
_____
_____

INTENTIONAL LEARNING:

_____
_____
_____
_____
_____
_____
_____

TIME	PM PLAN
12	
1	
2	
3	
4	
5	
6	
7	
8	
9	
10	
11	

DATE: _____

TODAY'S GOALS:

_____
_____
_____
_____
_____

MUST DO LIST:

_____
_____
_____
_____
_____
_____
_____

NOTES:

TIME	AM PLAN
12	
1	
2	
3	
4	
5	
6	
7	
8	
9	
10	
11	

_____
_____
_____
_____
_____
_____
_____

POWER-HOUR-INTENTIONS:

_____

_____

_____

_____

_____

_____

TODAYS WINS:

_____

_____

_____

_____

_____

_____

_____

INTENTIONAL LEARNING:

_____

_____

_____

_____

_____

_____

_____

_____

TIME	PM PLAN
12	
1	
2	
3	
4	
5	
6	
7	
8	
9	
10	
11	

DATE: _____

TODAY'S GOALS:

_____
_____
_____
_____

MUST DO LIST:

_____
_____
_____
_____
_____
_____
_____

NOTES:

TIME	AM PLAN
12	
1	
2	
3	
4	
5	
6	
7	
8	
9	
10	
11	

_____
_____
_____
_____
_____
_____
_____

POWER-HOUR-INTENTIONS:

_____

_____

_____

_____

_____

_____

TODAYS WINS:

_____

_____

_____

_____

_____

INTENTIONAL LEARNING:

_____

_____

_____

_____

_____

_____

TIME	PM PLAN
12	
1	
2	
3	
4	
5	
6	
7	
8	
9	
10	
11	

DATE: _____

TODAY'S GOALS:

_____
_____
_____
_____
_____

MUST DO LIST:

_____
_____
_____
_____
_____
_____
_____

NOTES:

TIME	AM PLAN
12	
1	
2	
3	
4	
5	
6	
7	
8	
9	
10	
11	

_____
_____
_____
_____
_____
_____
_____

POWER-HOUR-INTENTIONS:

_____
_____
_____
_____
_____
_____

TODAYS WINS:

_____
_____
_____
_____
_____
_____
_____

INTENTIONAL LEARNING:

_____
_____
_____
_____
_____
_____
_____
_____

TIME	PM PLAN
12	
1	
2	
3	
4	
5	
6	
7	
8	
9	
10	
11	

DATE: _____

TODAY'S GOALS:

_____
_____
_____
_____
_____

MUST DO LIST:

_____
_____
_____
_____
_____
_____
_____

NOTES:

TIME	AM PLAN
12	
1	
2	
3	
4	
5	
6	
7	
8	
9	
10	
11	

_____
_____
_____
_____
_____
_____
_____

POWER-HOUR-INTENTIONS:

_____
_____
_____
_____
_____
_____

TODAYS WINS:

_____
_____
_____
_____
_____
_____
_____

INTENTIONAL LEARNING:

_____
_____
_____
_____
_____
_____
_____
_____

TIME	PM PLAN
12	
1	
2	
3	
4	
5	
6	
7	
8	
9	
10	
11	

DATE: _____

TODAY'S GOALS:

_____

_____

_____

_____

_____

MUST DO LIST:

_____

_____

_____

_____

_____

_____

_____

_____

TIME	AM PLAN
12	
1	
2	
3	
4	
5	
6	
7	
8	
9	
10	
11	

NOTES:

_____

_____

_____

_____

_____

_____

_____

POWER-HOUR-INTENTIONS:

_____

_____

_____

_____

_____

_____

TODAYS WINS:

_____

_____

_____

_____

_____

_____

INTENTIONAL LEARNING:

_____

_____

_____

_____

_____

_____

_____

TIME	PM PLAN
12	
1	
2	
3	
4	
5	
6	
7	
8	
9	
10	
11	

DATE: _____

TODAY'S GOALS:

_____
_____
_____
_____
_____

MUST DO LIST:

_____
_____
_____
_____
_____
_____
_____

NOTES:

TIME	AM PLAN
12	
1	
2	
3	
4	
5	
6	
7	
8	
9	
10	
11	

_____
_____
_____
_____
_____
_____
_____

POWER-HOUR-INTENTIONS:

_____

_____

_____

_____

_____

TODAYS WINS:

_____

_____

_____

_____

_____

INTENTIONAL LEARNING:

_____

_____

_____

_____

_____

_____

TIME	PM PLAN
12	
1	
2	
3	
4	
5	
6	
7	
8	
9	
10	
11	

DATE: _____

TODAY'S GOALS:

_____
_____
_____
_____

MUST DO LIST:

_____
_____
_____
_____
_____
_____
_____

NOTES:

TIME	AM PLAN
12	
1	
2	
3	
4	
5	
6	
7	
8	
9	
10	
11	

_____
_____
_____
_____
_____
_____
_____

POWER-HOUR-INTENTIONS:

_____

_____

_____

_____

_____

TODAYS WINS:

_____

_____

_____

_____

_____

_____

INTENTIONAL LEARNING:

_____

_____

_____

_____

_____

_____

_____

TIME	PM PLAN
12	
1	
2	
3	
4	
5	
6	
7	
8	
9	
10	
11	

DATE: _____

TODAY'S GOALS:

_____
_____
_____
_____
_____

MUST DO LIST:

_____
_____
_____
_____
_____
_____
_____

NOTES:

_____
_____
_____
_____
_____
_____
_____

TIME	AM PLAN
12	
1	
2	
3	
4	
5	
6	
7	
8	
9	
10	
11	

POWER-HOUR-INTENTIONS:

_____

_____

_____

_____

_____

_____

TODAYS WINS:

_____

_____

_____

_____

_____

INTENTIONAL LEARNING:

_____

_____

_____

_____

_____

_____

_____

TIME	PM PLAN
12	
1	
2	
3	
4	
5	
6	
7	
8	
9	
10	
11	

DATE: _____

TODAY'S GOALS:

_____
_____
_____
_____

MUST DO LIST:

_____
_____
_____
_____
_____
_____
_____

NOTES:

TIME	AM PLAN
12	
1	
2	
3	
4	
5	
6	
7	
8	
9	
10	
11	

_____
_____
_____
_____
_____
_____
_____

POWER-HOUR-INTENTIONS:

_____
_____
_____
_____
_____
_____

TODAYS WINS:

_____
_____
_____
_____
_____
_____
_____

INTENTIONAL LEARNING:

_____
_____
_____
_____
_____
_____
_____
_____

TIME	PM PLAN
12	
1	
2	
3	
4	
5	
6	
7	
8	
9	
10	
11	

DATE: _____

TODAY'S GOALS:

_____

_____

_____

_____

MUST DO LIST:

_____

_____

_____

_____

_____

_____

_____

NOTES:

TIME	AM PLAN
12	
1	
2	
3	
4	
5	
6	
7	
8	
9	
10	
11	

_____

_____

_____

_____

_____

_____

_____

POWER-HOUR-INTENTIONS:

_____

_____

_____

_____

_____

TODAYS WINS:

_____

_____

_____

_____

_____

INTENTIONAL LEARNING:

_____

_____

_____

_____

_____

_____

TIME	PM PLAN
12	
1	
2	
3	
4	
5	
6	
7	
8	
9	
10	
11	

DATE: _____

TODAY'S GOALS:

_____
_____
_____
_____
_____

MUST DO LIST:

_____
_____
_____
_____
_____
_____
_____

NOTES:

_____
_____
_____
_____
_____
_____
_____

TIME	AM PLAN
12	
1	
2	
3	
4	
5	
6	
7	
8	
9	
10	
11	

POWER-HOUR-INTENTIONS:

_____

_____

_____

_____

_____

_____

TODAYS WINS:

_____

_____

_____

_____

_____

_____

INTENTIONAL LEARNING:

_____

_____

_____

_____

_____

_____

_____

TIME	PM PLAN
12	
1	
2	
3	
4	
5	
6	
7	
8	
9	
10	
11	

DATE: _____

TODAY'S GOALS:

_____
_____
_____
_____
_____

MUST DO LIST:

_____
_____
_____
_____
_____
_____

NOTES:

_____
_____
_____
_____
_____
_____
_____

TIME	AM PLAN
12	
1	
2	
3	
4	
5	
6	
7	
8	
9	
10	
11	

POWER-HOUR-INTENTIONS:

_____
_____
_____
_____
_____
_____

TODAYS WINS:

TIME	PM PLAN
12	
1	
2	
3	
4	
5	
6	
7	
8	
9	
10	
11	

INTENTIONAL LEARNING:

DATE: _____

TODAY'S GOALS:

_____

_____

_____

_____

_____

MUST DO LIST:

_____

_____

_____

_____

_____

_____

_____

NOTES:

TIME	AM PLAN
12	
1	
2	
3	
4	
5	
6	
7	
8	
9	
10	
11	

_____

_____

_____

_____

_____

_____

POWER-HOUR-INTENTIONS:

_____
_____
_____
_____
_____
_____

TODAYS WINS:

_____
_____
_____
_____
_____
_____

INTENTIONAL LEARNING:

_____
_____
_____
_____
_____
_____
_____

TIME	PM PLAN
12	
1	
2	
3	
4	
5	
6	
7	
8	
9	
10	
11	

DATE: _____

TODAY'S GOALS:

_____
_____
_____
_____
_____

MUST DO LIST:

_____
_____
_____
_____
_____
_____
_____

NOTES:

TIME	AM PLAN
12	
1	
2	
3	
4	
5	
6	
7	
8	
9	
10	
11	

_____
_____
_____
_____
_____
_____
_____

POWER-HOUR-INTENTIONS:

_____
_____
_____
_____
_____
_____

TODAYS WINS:

_____
_____
_____
_____
_____
_____

INTENTIONAL LEARNING:

_____
_____
_____
_____
_____
_____

TIME	PM PLAN
12	
1	
2	
3	
4	
5	
6	
7	
8	
9	
10	
11	

DATE: _____

TODAY'S GOALS:

_____

_____

_____

_____

MUST DO LIST:

_____

_____

_____

_____

_____

_____

NOTES:

_____

_____

_____

_____

_____

_____

TIME	AM PLAN
12	
1	
2	
3	
4	
5	
6	
7	
8	
9	
10	
11	

POWER-HOUR-INTENTIONS:

_____

_____

_____

_____

_____

TODAYS WINS:

_____

_____

_____

_____

_____

_____

INTENTIONAL LEARNING:

_____

_____

_____

_____

_____

_____

TIME	PM PLAN
12	
1	
2	
3	
4	
5	
6	
7	
8	
9	
10	
11	

DATE: _____

TODAY'S GOALS:

_____
_____
_____
_____
_____

MUST DO LIST:

_____
_____
_____
_____
_____
_____
_____
_____

NOTES:

TIME	AM PLAN
12	
1	
2	
3	
4	
5	
6	
7	
8	
9	
10	
11	

_____
_____
_____
_____
_____
_____

POWER-HOUR-INTENTIONS:

_____

_____

_____

_____

_____

_____

TODAYS WINS:

_____

_____

_____

_____

_____

_____

INTENTIONAL LEARNING:

_____

_____

_____

_____

_____

_____

_____

TIME	PM PLAN
12	
1	
2	
3	
4	
5	
6	
7	
8	
9	
10	
11	

DATE: _____

TODAY'S GOALS:

_____
_____
_____
_____
_____

MUST DO LIST:

_____
_____
_____
_____
_____
_____
_____

NOTES

TIME	AM PLAN
12	
1	
2	
3	
4	
5	
6	
7	
8	
9	
10	
11	

_____
_____
_____
_____
_____
_____
_____

POWER-HOUR-INTENTIONS

_____
_____
_____
_____
_____
_____
_____

TODAYS WINS:

_____
_____
_____
_____
_____
_____

INTENTIONAL LEARNING:

_____
_____
_____
_____
_____
_____
_____

TIME	PM PLAN
12	
1	
2	
3	
4	
5	
6	
7	
8	
9	
10	
11	

DATE: _____

TODAY'S GOALS:

_____
_____
_____
_____
_____

MUST DO LIST:

_____
_____
_____
_____
_____
_____
_____

NOTES:

TIME	AM PLAN
12	
1	
2	
3	
4	
5	
6	
7	
8	
9	
10	
11	

_____
_____
_____
_____
_____
_____

POWER-HOUR-INTENTIONS:

_____
_____
_____
_____
_____
_____
_____

TODAYS WINS:

_____
_____
_____
_____
_____
_____

INTENTIONAL LEARNING:

_____
_____
_____
_____
_____
_____

TIME	PM PLAN
12	
1	
2	
3	
4	
5	
6	
7	
8	
9	
10	
11	

DATE: _____

TODAY'S GOALS:

_____
_____
_____
_____
_____

MUST DO LIST:

_____
_____
_____
_____
_____
_____

NOTES

_____
_____
_____
_____
_____
_____

TIME	AM PLAN
12	
1	
2	
3	
4	
5	
6	
7	
8	
9	
10	
11	

POWER-HOUR-INTENTIONS

_____
_____
_____
_____
_____
_____
_____

TODAYS WINS:

_____
_____
_____
_____
_____

INTENTIONAL LEARNING:

_____
_____
_____
_____
_____
_____
_____

TIME	PM PLAN
12	
1	
2	
3	
4	
5	
6	
7	
8	
9	
10	
11	

DATE: _____

TODAY'S GOALS:

_____
_____
_____
_____
_____
_____

MUST DO LIST:

_____
_____
_____
_____
_____
_____
_____

TIME	AM PLAN
12	
1	
2	
3	
4	
5	
6	
7	
8	
9	
10	
11	

NOTES

_____
_____
_____
_____
_____
_____
_____

POWER-HOUR-INTENTIONS

_____
_____
_____
_____
_____
_____
_____
_____

TODAYS WINS:

_____
_____
_____
_____
_____
_____

INTENTIONAL LEARNING:

_____
_____
_____
_____
_____
_____
_____
_____
_____

TIME	PM PLAN
12	
1	
2	
3	
4	
5	
6	
7	
8	
9	
10	
11	

DATE: _____

TODAY'S GOALS:

_____

_____

_____

_____

_____

MUST DO LIST:

_____

_____

_____

_____

_____

_____

NOTES

_____

TIME	AM PLAN
12	
1	
2	
3	
4	
5	
6	
7	
8	
9	
10	
11	

_____

_____

_____

_____

_____

_____

_____

_____

POWER-HOUR-INTENTIONS:

_____

_____

_____

_____

_____

_____

_____

TODAYS WINS:

_____

_____

_____

_____

_____

INTENTIONAL LEARNING:

_____

_____

_____

_____

_____

_____

_____

TIME	PM PLAN
12	
1	
2	
3	
4	
5	
6	
7	
8	
9	
10	
11	

DATE: _____

TODAY'S GOALS:

_____
_____
_____
_____
_____

MUST DO LIST:

_____
_____
_____
_____
_____
_____
_____

TIME	AM PLAN
12	
1	
2	
3	
4	
5	
6	
7	
8	
9	
10	
11	

NOTES

_____
_____
_____
_____
_____
_____
_____

POWER-HOUR-INTENTIONS

_____
_____
_____
_____
_____
_____
_____

TODAYS WINS:

_____
_____
_____
_____
_____
_____

INTENTIONAL LEARNING:

_____
_____
_____
_____
_____
_____
_____

TIME	PM PLAN
12	
1	
2	
3	
4	
5	
6	
7	
8	
9	
10	
11	

DATE: _____

TODAY'S GOALS:

_____
_____
_____
_____
_____
_____

MUST DO LIST:

_____
_____
_____
_____
_____
_____
_____

NOTES

_____
_____
_____
_____
_____
_____
_____

TIME	AM PLAN
12	
1	
2	
3	
4	
5	
6	
7	
8	
9	
10	
11	

POWER-HOUR-INTENTIONS

_____

_____

_____

_____

_____

_____

_____

TODAYS WINS:

_____

_____

_____

_____

_____

_____

INTENTIONAL LEARNING:

_____

_____

_____

_____

_____

_____

TIME	PM PLAN
12	
1	
2	
3	
4	
5	
6	
7	
8	
9	
10	
11	

DATE: _____

TODAY'S GOALS:

_____
_____
_____
_____
_____

MUST DO LIST:

_____
_____
_____
_____
_____
_____
_____

TIME	AM PLAN
12	
1	
2	
3	
4	
5	
6	
7	
8	
9	
10	
11	

NOTES

_____
_____
_____
_____
_____
_____
_____

POWER-HOUR-INTENTIONS

_____
_____
_____
_____
_____
_____
_____

TODAYS WINS:

_____
_____
_____
_____
_____

INTENTIONAL LEARNING:

_____
_____
_____
_____
_____
_____

TIME	PM PLAN
12	
1	
2	
3	
4	
5	
6	
7	
8	
9	
10	
11	

DATE: _____

TODAY'S GOALS:

_____
_____
_____
_____
_____
_____

MUST DO LIST:

_____
_____
_____
_____
_____
_____
_____

TIME	AM PLAN
12	
1	
2	
3	
4	
5	
6	
7	
8	
9	
10	
11	

NOTES

_____
_____
_____
_____
_____
_____
_____

POWER-HOUR-INTENTIONS

_____

_____

_____

_____

_____

_____

_____

TODAYS WINS:

_____

_____

_____

_____

_____

INTENTIONAL LEARNING:

_____

_____

_____

_____

_____

_____

TIME	PM PLAN
12	
1	
2	
3	
4	
5	
6	
7	
8	
9	
10	
11	

Achievements

Date	Achievement	Reward

To Be Read List

Book Title	Author	Genre

DAILY HABIT TRACKER
"We are what we repeatedly do"

This is a weekly habit tracker that allows you to keep track of how many times you are participating in healthy habits leading you closer to your goals. Identify 5 daily habits that will push you closer to your goals. Next work on implementing them daily for the next three months. Some examples of habits that I implemented daily included; saying affirmations, reading, participating in my daily power hour. I also did a lot of self-care activities because the truth is, if you're nor fueling your body you will not have the energy you need to be successful. You can consider setting healthy habits on this tracker such as drinking 64 ounces of water, getting 8 hours of sleep or working out. These are just some suggestions please make sure you're identifying habits that you also believe will help you on this journey. When you first begin you may not be implementing these habits daily. The goal is that you are practicing these healthy habits with more frequency during your writing journey and beyond.

Week 1

My Habit	Sunday	Monday	Tuesday	Wednesday	Thursday	Friday	Saturday

Week 2

My Habit	Sunday	Monday	Tuesday	Wednesday	Thursday	Friday	Saturday

Week 3

My Habit	Sunday	Monday	Tuesday	Wednesday	Thursday	Friday	Saturday

Week 4

My Habit	Sunday	Monday	Tuesday	Wednesday	Thursday	Friday	Saturday

Week 5

My Habit	Sunday	Monday	Tuesday	Wednesday	Thursday	Friday	Saturday

Week 6

My Habit	Sunday	Monday	Tuesday	Wednesday	Thursday	Friday	Saturday

Week 7

My Habit	Sunday	Monday	Tuesday	Wednesday	Thursday	Friday	Saturday

Week 8

My Habit	Sunday	Monday	Tuesday	Wednesday	Thursday	Friday	Saturday

Week 9

My Habit	Sunday	Monday	Tuesday	Wednesday	Thursday	Friday	Saturday

Week 10

My Habit	Sunday	Monday	Tuesday	Wednesday	Thursday	Friday	Saturday

Week 11

My Habit	Sunday	Monday	Tuesday	Wednesday	Thursday	Friday	Saturday

Week 12

My Habit	Sunday	Monday	Tuesday	Wednesday	Thursday	Friday	Saturday

Reflection Section

1. **What did you accomplish over the last three months?**

2. **What is your biggest takeaway?**

3. **What will you be working on going forward?**

POWERFUL AFFIRMATIVE STATEMENTS

Affirmations are sentences aimed to affect the conscious and the subconscious mind in a positive way Affirmations are used to motivate you and help you to keep your mind focused on the goals you desire to achieve. Pick one affirmation from below, or a personal one. Repeat the affirmation once in the morning, afternoon and evening at bare minimum. When you say it, say it as though it is already done. You can also feel free to read these all during the day. These positive affirmations will help you to feel positive, energetic and active, and therefore, put you in a better position to succeed by transforming your inner and external worlds.

- *I deserve to be happy and successful*

- *I am worthy of respect*

- *I embrace my differences since I was made to be unique*

- *I have the power to change myself*

- *I can <u>forgive and understand others</u> and their motives*

- *I can make my own choices and decisions*

- *I am free to choose to live as I wish and to give priority to my desires*

- *I can choose happiness whenever I wish no matter what my circumstances*

- *I am flexible and open to change in every aspect of my life*

- *I act with confidence having a general plan and accept plans are open to Alteration*

- *It is enough to have done my best*

- *I deserve to be loved*

- *I accept myself just as I am*

- *I will continue to learn and grow*

- *Mistakes are just stepping stones to my achievement*

- I deserve a good life. I deny any need for suffering and misery.

- *I am competent, smart and able*

- *I am changing for the better*

- *I have great ideas and make powerful contributions*

- *I am confident with my life plan and the way in which things are going*

- *My dreams and goals matter*

- *I can quickly get all of the knowledge I need to succeed*

- *I let go of negative thinking*

- *I surround myself with people who bring out the best in me*

- *I am congruent in everything I say and do*

- *I recognize the many good qualities that I have*

- I am courageous. I am willing to act in spite of any fear.

- I am positive and optimistic. I believe things will always work out for the best.

- I am successful right now

- I am always looking for ways to grow